# Do I UNDERSTAND My Child?

**Do I really understand myself?**

**Do I really understand my child?**

**How may I know?**

By

## Olen Holderby

## Truth
### Publications

*Taking His hand,*
*Helping each other home.*
™

ISBN 10: 1-58427-327-5
ISBN 13: 978-158427-327-1

First Printing: 2011

**Truth Publications, Inc.**
**CEI Bookstore**
**220 S. Marion St., Athens, AL 35611**
**855-492-6657**
**sales@truthpublications.com**
**www.truthbooks.com**

# TABLE OF CONTENTS

# DEDICATION

To that host of dedicated parents who sincerely desire to be more effective as parents and more productive as children of God, who desire to see their own children grow into contributing citizens of society and assets to the Cause of Christ.

# PREFACE

We are living in a period of almost perfect means, but with confused ends. The lack of planned and proper goals of life are so obvious that proof need not be offered. Live, for many, has become a "rat race" without knowing just where the finish line is to be found. Rushing, rushing, but going nowhere! The home has not escaped this rush of uncertainty and instability.

Many parents do not understand nor do they appear to be too concerned about their children. Love, understanding, and respect are rare ingredients in just too many homes. This is, of course, the opposite of what God would have it be. Parents need to know that children are gifts of God (Gen. 33:5; 48:9). God has charged parents with the responsibility of molding these gifts into a certain type of personality, suitable to Him (Eph. 6:4; Col.3:21).

This book is planned in an effort to assist parents to that end. UNDERSTANDING is the main thesis of this work. I have resisted the temptation toward the writing of much detail; with the exception of Chapter IX, I have greatly condensed my material in an effort to make this work more practical and accessible. I have avoided the use of technical terms as much as possible, aiming to make the points easily understood. It is hoped that you will find this work profitable in discharging your responsibility as a parent.

Olen Holderby

# Chapter 1

# THE NEED

The need for a better understanding of ourselves of our children, and of others is so obvious that little need be said to establish this as an accepted fact. Perhaps the following examples will serve some purpose in helping the reader to see that there is a very real need for a better understanding of all with whom we have to do.

Jane almost constantly bragged about herself and often remarked, "I have to, my husband never says anything good about me." "He must be a lousy husband," remarked her friend, "to not appreciate you any more than that."

"Why do my children act that way?" a parent is heard to remark. And another, "Why did my son turn to crime?" "I just don't know why Alice does not become a Christian," said her mother. "My children will hate me if I punish them as my wife wants me to do," remarks one worried father. "He is so rebellious, and my other two gave me no difficulty at all." "I wished my children all behaved as well as yours." "If that little demon was mine, I'd teach him a thing or two." Do these statements sound familiar?

Susan had filed for divorce, declaring, "We just cannot get along!" Her husband retorted, "We will get along when you want to get along!" "My wife's housekeeping is terrible. Her mother wasn't that way, why is she?" remarked a husband who had begun spending more time away from home. One wife was heard to say, "If my husband was the manager that my father was, we would have more happiness in the home." "Marriage is just not what I expected it to be." Do any of these statements have any similarity with what you have heard?

One young lady said more than she may have thought when she said, "My parents are my biggest problem." "I came to you because I can't talk to my parents; they don't understand me." "My dad never does anything with me; he just does not have time." "My mother says she hates me because I remind her of my father." What a sad commentary it is on parents for youngsters to be able to honestly make such statements!

In tears, parents are often heard to remark of their failures in rearing their children. No greater charge was ever assigned to parents than that contained in Ephesians 6:4, "And, ye fathers, provoke not your children to wrath; but bring them up in the nurture and admonition of the Lord." Yet, we see so many well-meaning and good-intentioned parents falling far short of this demand. Why is this so? All who are familiar with the New Testament will be quick to recognize the Scriptures as the perfect pattern in all that God demands of us (James 1:25; 2 Tim. 3:16-17). Why is it that so many fail in the application of this perfect pattern? I am convinced that one of the main reasons for this failure is a lack of understanding of our children. At best we shall make mistakes, but why should we not endeavor to reduce these mistakes and, thus, give our children a better chance at growing up and becoming good Christians and contributing citizens of the society in which they live?

Gospel preachers often fail in solving problems related to the church, or fail in reaching certain people with the truth. Why? Elders often fail in maintaining good working relationships with members of the local church. Why? Could these reasons be the same as for the failure of many parents—simply not understanding the people with whom they are to work? In Colossians 4:6 the Apostle Paul places some emphasis on the "how" of answering others. Dealing with someone must be opportune as regards to time and person. What we have to say should be suited to the particular person, adapted to meet the needs of the moment. How can this be done without some understanding of the person? One thought often quoted, Proverbs 22:6 ("Train up a child in the way he should go: and when he is old, he will not depart from it"), can be a resource by considering the marginal reading—"in his way." Could it be that we try to teach our children as if they were already adults? Would it not be wise to train them "as a child"? Surely we can see that there is a difference.

One's right to a formal education is to be found in the willingness to use that education to the glory of God. This design is often defeated in the public school systems, with infidel and atheistic teachers and professors offering their unproven theories and ridiculing the Bible as if it was a product of fallible man. This is especially true on the secondary and college level, though such is found as early as in the kindergarten or first grade. It can be easily seen, then, just how important it really is for children to approach those trying years with a good foundation in God's Word. Much can be learned from the areas of Psychology and Sociology that are real assets to our effectiveness as Christians. However, it is, indeed, a sad situation when a student is not able to "weed out" that part which is without virtue; and, to retain that part which can serve him well as a servant of God.

In any study, one of the most difficult things to do is to get people to accept facts, especially when these facts are personal in nature and cause some degree of discomfort. It appears that we just don't like to apply such facts to ourselves! If you are prepared to look facts straight in the face, then the following chapters will be profitable to you. This assumes, of course, that you are not mentally lazy and you are willing to apply these things to yourself. Your efforts herein can make the difference between whether your life is sunshine or shadows.[1] As you pursue this material, it is suggested that you endeavor to obtain a better understanding of:

| | |
|---|---|
| **Yourself** | Why do you think as you do? |
| | Why do you react to certain things as you do? |
| | In short, what makes you tick? |
| **Your Children** | Why do they behave as they do? |
| | Why or how did they develop certain attitudes? |
| | What danger signals can you see in their behavior? |
| | Again, in short, what makes them tick? |

---

[1] "Very little is needed to make a happy life. It is all within yourself, in your way of thinking." —Marcus Aurelius. Cf. Philippians 4:8.

# Chapter 2

# IT ALL BEGINS AT BIRTH

Passing over the conception and materialization in the womb, we come directly to our topic, as it begins at the time of birth. Every normal person has the same psychological make-up at the time of birth. The following picture will help explain.

| #2 | The environmental, learned experiences, the parental do's and don'ts |
|---|---|
| Ego | Yourself, as you think of yourself |
| #3 | Heredity, storehouse of all primitive instincts and natural desires |

It would appear to be worthwhile to offer some brief comments on the above picture.

**#3:** When one is born, he is in possession of these natural desires. Such desires as to eat, to drink, for comfort, for love, for sex, and even for survival are all present. In short, the baby is in possession of all the desires that would cause him to act in a more or less animalistic way.

**#2:** this area is vacant at birth, and will be filled by the youngster's experiences and what he is taught. This teaching and the experiences may be good or bad; either may fill this vacancy.

**Ego:** This is yourself. The ego acts to protect itself; it is self-preservative, *first, last,* and *always.*

Let's rearrange this picture and take a second look (next page), seeing the great importance—as we notice some of the functions.

```
┌──────────┐
│   # 2    │────────────────┐ Parental Do's & Don'ts │
├──────────┤           ╲ ╱ ↗                         ↓
│   Ego    │────────────╳──── (Mediator) --- Conflicts
├──────────┤           ╱ ╲ ↘                         ↑
│   # 3    │────────────────┘ Natural Desires        │
└──────────┘
```

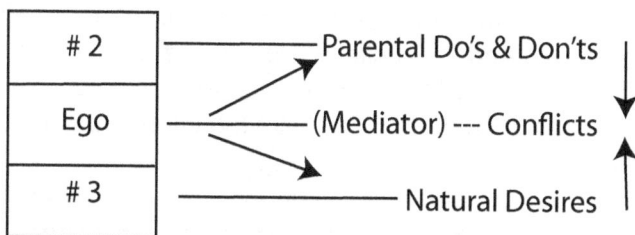

As a baby begins to grow, he has certain learning experiences. This training may prove to be in direct conflict with his natural desires. When the *conflict* occurs, the child is going to move either toward area #3 with its natural desires or will move toward area #2 with its imposed do's and don'ts. Now, which way will he go? He will move toward which ever area is the stronger! PARENTS, right here is the focal point of this brief chapter; *the importance of early and proper training.* The awesome task before parents is to see to it that their children have adequate training to offset the tendency to follow the natural desires. We will view conflicts a little more in a future chapter; but, there is another point or two which become important here.

If the *conflict* is not resolved or temporarily satisfied it can lead to a disintegration of the ego, or a mental teardown. This is true in children or adults. However, keep in mind that what an adult may consider a trivial matter may well be a matter of extreme importance to the child. Here is where *stress* or *pressure* enters the picture, for *stress* is the result of unresolved conflicts. The ability to stand *stress* is in the ego; and everyone has what is called a stress-toleration-point, a point at which one begins to depart from what otherwise would be his normal behavior. The last picture shows the Ego as a mediator between #3 and #2, trying to resolve the conflicts which develop. This is its natural function, but this function depends upon the training and experiences brought to bear on the youngster. Here, again, we see the important role of the parents.

Conflicts (thus Stress) arise from different sources. Any amount of Stress may be *internal* or it may be *external.* To be internal is to say that the conflict or stress is from within the individual—mental, emotional, psychological, etc. To be external is to say that it comes from outside the individual—sociological, or pressure brought to bear because of some outside person or thing. When a goal in an individual's life is blocked he experiences *frustration*. The same is true when a need is blocked. From these brief comments you should be able to see the close relationship of the terms: Conflict, Stress, and Frustration. Let's illustrate the internal/external aspects of conflicts:

| Conflicts | |
|---|---|
| **Internal** | **External** |
| Desire vs. Desire | Things |
| Love vs. Desire | People |
| Love vs. Love | Authority Standards |
| Etc. | Etc. |

All our life we shall experience conflicts; as rapidly as one is resolved another is quite ready to take its place. We cannot avoid this. However, we can prepare ourselves to deal with such conflicts, and likewise prepare our children. The resolving of a conflict is a step further toward maturity. How pleased parents must be to witness their youngsters assuming the responsibility of properly resolving the conflicts in their lives![2] The Christian may turn to Christ to resolve these conflicts (Rom. 7:21-25).

---

[2] "Everything has its beauty; but not everyone sees it." —Confucius

# Chapter 3

# TERMS OF IMPORTANCE

The following terms are briefly discussed because of their common usage and because of their direct bearing on the subject at hand: Understanding!

**Personality:** Referring back to Chapter II, I suggest personality is a combination of Environment, Ego, Heredity. In other words "your" personality is you—all of you. Many speak of personality as if, like our pants, we put it off at night and on in the morning. However, the personality is the pants which you wear all the time. The way you talk, the way you walk, the way you comb your hair, etc. are all included in the term personality. Now what must you do in order to change the personality? The personality will change just to the extent that you change. Personality is a very inclusive term. Perhaps I can illustrate with the following picture:

## Personality

Behavior, Interests, Health, Attitudes, Sociability, Emotions, Achievements, Physical Appearance, Heredity, Character, Integrity, Etc.

Outside Factors Often Affecting Personality
1. Experiences (all the time)
2. Events (observed)
3. Socio—Economic (culture)
4. Peer Groups
5. Education
6. Security Giving Factors
7. Adequacy—giving Experiences
8. Siblings

You will notice that *behavior* is a part of the personality. Behavior is seen as the function (together) of Heredity (#3) and Environment (#2) (see chart on p. 10). You will also notice that *character* is a part of personality; and character is usually thought of as having moral attributes. Our morals, then, are seen as a part of the personality. I trust that as brief as this may be, it shall show just how very inclusive personality remains. The "outside factors often affecting personality" is not a complete list, but are mere samples, showing some of the forces that are brought to bear to make us what we are—a distinct personality.

**Hallucinations:** This is the act of seeing, hearing, feeling, tasting, or smelling that which is not there.

**Delusions:** This is the act of persistently believing something to be a fact despite the evidence to the contrary. Both delusions and hallucinations may be observed in small children as they move through the age of "tall tales." However, should either persist beyond the age of seven or eight years, it should be taken as a danger signal and your doctor should be consulted.

**Hypochondriac:** One who has obsessive concern for his health without a logical set of symptoms. This concern most often manifests itself by the person running from one doctor to another in an effort to discover just what his illness may be. He may eventually find one who will tell him that something is wrong with him; then, of course, all the previous doctors suddenly become "quacks." Seldom do we find a hypochondriac among youngsters. However, when you find one, quite often you will find behind all this a *parental over—concern* for that person's health when he was a youngster.

**Anxiety:** Basically this is a fear of that which is unknown. Anxiety has also been spoken of as fear directed inwardly; and, often the person cannot explain his fear. Anxiety may be broken down into four different kinds of fear:

1. Fear of the unknown (think of the noises which we may hear in the dark)

2. Fear attached to naught (scared, but doesn't know why he is scared)

3. Fear attached to something (a history of cancer in our family)

4. Fear of separation (a youngster going to school for the first time or a man about to lose his job)

Anxiety can usually be lessened by encouraging the person to externalize his interests, to think about things outside himself.

**Maturity:** The ability to postpone present pleasures for later gains. This is what parents are doing when they encourage a child to get an education before going to work on a regular basis. Further, this is what true Christianity is all about. In the context of this definition, how many of us can honestly say we are mature? Does this not suggest that maturing is a continuing process? Apply this definition to the different areas of your life and see what I mean.

**Grown-up:** This expression is often used in the same way the word *maturity* is used. Let me suggest a meaning: The ability to handle the problems of life constructively. This definition suggests nothing with regards to age. Like *maturity*, this is seen as a continuing process. We make a mistake by equating *maturity* or *grown-up* with a particular chronological age.

The giving of these few terms and the brief comments upon each will, I trust, make some contribution to your understanding and use of them. As in other portions of this work, I suggest that you try to see yourself in the application of these terms. It is not always pleasant for one to be factual and honest about one's self.[3]

---

[3] "Sorrow knocked at the door, Faith answered, and found no one there."
— Japanese Proverb

# Chapter 4

# ATTITUDES AND CONFLICTS

## Attitudes

*Attitudes are set by training and experience*, and are composed of at least three different kinds:

1. Reality Attitude: One's ideas of how he thinks things really are.

2. Ethical Attitude: A person's ideas of right or wrong.

3. Fantasy Attitude: Based on what one thinks he would like to be, or on the way he would like things to be.

The names of these attitudes are not important, but the ideas are important. Remember that, in each case, one's attitude is always determined by that one's training and experience. This thought will come in for more discussion when we get to discussing the child. Attitudes may also be divided into two different kinds, as given below with some examples:

In Luke 16:8, Jesus said, ". . . the children of this world are in their generation wiser than the children of light." Our Lord here stated a fact. But, I ask, "Why must this be so?" Jesus didn't make this so, neither did God so determine it to be so. It was, nonetheless, a fact and Jesus so stated it. Have you ever heard such statements as: "Why isn't he more receptive to the truth?" Or, "Why am I not more successful in reaching others with the truth?" Again, "I know the truth, I can teach the truth, why am I not more successful?" Could the fault be with us? Maybe we need to follow the advice offered by Paul in 2 Corinthians 13:5, and closely examine ourselves. Would not this also be so with reference to teaching or rearing our children?

| CONSTRUCTIVE ATTITUDES | | DESTRUCTIVE ATTITUDES |
|---|---|---|
| 1. Willingness to accept reality | | 1. Unwillingness to accept reality |
| 2. Flexibility | | 2. Rigid (not easily adapted) |
| 3. Unselfish love | | 3. Selfish or hate |
| 4. Use our intelligence | | 4. Not use our intelligence |
| 5. Tolerance | | 5. Intolerance |
| 6. Patience | **You** | 6. Impatience |
| 7. Integrity (self-respect) | **Make** | 7. Dishonest (fear, anger) |
| 8. Understanding | **The** | 8. Resentment |
| 9. Kindness | **Choice** | 9. Begrudging |
| 10. Humility | | 10. Irritation and annoyed |
| 11. Loyalty | | 11. Rebellion and aggressive |
| 12. Courage | | 12. Discouragement |
| 13. Optimism | | 13. Pessimism, anxiety, envy, jealousy |
| 14. Sense of Humor | | 14. Guilt, shame, etc. |
| 15. Trusting | | 15. Suspicious |
| 16. Forgiveness | | 16. Demanding |

Please read Titus 2:11-12. The word "soberly" directs our attention inward and deals with our attitude toward ourselves. The word "righteously" deals with our attitude toward our fellow man, for God's righteousness is expressed from man to man. The word "godly" deals with our relationship and attitude toward God. Here, then, we are commanded to examine our attitudes in the various relationships of our life. Attitudes do not have to be permanent. Since attitudes are set by training and experience, the way to change the attitude is to offer better training and more wholesome experiences. The parent has basic responsibility for this with the child. The precious little time that we have them with us results in very little time to waste.

## Conflicts

A brief review of Chapter II will reintroduce you to the subject of conflicts. To get right at our subject, let me introduce you to a chart of some examples of common conflicts:

| | vs. | |
|---|---|---|
| 1. Dependence | | 1. Independence |
| 2. Smoking | | 2. Not to Smoke |
| 3. Obey Parents | | 3. Not to Obey |
| 4. To be Married | **You** | 4. Not to be Married |
| 5. To Have Children | | 5. Have no Children |
| 6. Dieting | **Must** | 6. Eating |
| 7. Drinking Alcoholic Drinks | **Make** | 7. Not Drinking |
| 8. Life | | 8. Death |
| 9. Employee | **The** | 9. Employer |
| 10. Staying With My Job | | 10. Changing Jobs |
| 11. Going to College | **Choice!** | 11. Not Going to College |
| 12. Being Truthful | | 12. Being Untruthful |

When these or other conflicts arise, remember that we shall move in the direction that is the stronger—Our Training or Our Natural Desires. This natural desire is often referred to as the "course of least resistance." *Unless* one is properly trained, wisdom plays little part in the choice that usually is made. We may sum up this cause for conflicts by saying that they are caused by incompatible desires, needs, or environmental demands. Conflicts are not always easily understood, they simply are not just "cut and dried" decisions to be made.

In order to better understand how conflicts may work, let's notice two or three kinds. One may desire to do something, but want to avoid the responsibility attached. When one must decide between two things that he wants this is another type of conflict. Then, there are times when one wants two different things but wants to avoid the uncomfortable aspects of those things. These thoughts are introduced to merely show that conflicts can sometimes get to be complicated. Most people are not able to immediately resolve conflicts that arise, but *all* people react to every conflict.

## How Do We React To Conflicts?

Two previously mentioned facts should be remembered: The ego is the mediator, and the ego acts to defend itself—it is self-protective always. How does this ego defend itself when conflicts arise? There is a rather lengthy list of what are called Ego-Defense Mechanisms, but, just a few mentioned here will offer some understanding of the process:

1. **Rationalization.** The teenager excitedly requested her mother's permission to attend a "sleep-over." The mother's reply was a firm, "No!" After some moments of hesitation, the young lady left the room and was heard saying, "I didn't want to go anyway." She was reacting to the sudden conflict, and in a way that permitted her to tolerate the situation.

2. **Denial of Reality.** Just telling one's self that there is no problem, no conflict. "Not really!"

3. **Compensation.** Substituting something else that, for the moment, takes the mind off the conflict.

4. **Emotional Isolation.** Because of the strong feelings that are often involved in conflicts, there are those who react by pulling within themselves, holding their feelings inside and not talking with anyone about such feelings.

5. **Fantasies.** Here one's imagination goes to work; he lives in somewhat of a dream-world – thus projecting himself into the situation which he really wanted, or projecting himself completely out of the conflicting situation.

6. **Identification.** This is when we identify ourselves with another person who has experienced the same thing, thus finding some emotional comfort in our unwanted position.

7. **Regression.** Here we find a person pushing the problem into the background, so as not to think on it. This is done consciously.

8. **Repression.** The same as regression, but is unconsciously done, the individual acting without realizing what he is doing.

I want to emphasize the use of these defense mechanisms is not bad. In fact it is good if—and this is a big *if*—they do not become crutches to us, if they are not over—used. Remember that we said all conflicts must be resolved, but we did not say immediately! These defense mechanisms are good for temporary use, until time and circumstances permit a better solution. Should any of these become *crutches* to us, they will also become problems—within themselves.

Thus, our situation would become more difficult to cope with. Do not permit a conflict to go long unresolved! Seek help if need be! Your own emotional health is at stake!

If you wish to reflect upon one of the most outstanding areas of conflicts, think on your own efforts at getting someone to become a Christian, or persuading an unfaithful member of the church to repent. What keeps him from following your advice? Conflicts? It, of course, is your job to help remove or resolve those conflicts so that such people will act wisely. Having seen this, can we not see the same responsibility parents have, with reference to our children?

# Chapter 5

# PSYCHOLOGICAL STAGES OF GROWTH

In this brief chapter we are concerned with the five psychological stages of growth, as we move through life – from birth to adulthood. Those are:

1. Oral
2. Anal
3. Genital
4. Homosexual
5. Heterosexual

**Oral:** This stage begins at birth and is commonly referred to as the "sucking stage." The mother is one great big breast to the infant. He may, as time goes on, associate the mother's face and caresses with the feeding. And, of course, this small realm continues to enlarge. His drives and needs are centered on what goes into his mouth and his bodily comfort. Just about everything must be tried by sticking it in his mouth.

**Anal:** There is not a distinct line between any two of these stages, but the change can be observed. Here we begin to see the youngster learn bowl control, even if he does so just to please his mother, at the beginning. He will be learning to manipulate himself, crawling, walking, etc. It might be added that this is also the stage when the youngster will normally have a great deal of self-curiosity. He is fascinated by the different parts of his body.

**Genital:** Here we see that self-curiosity carried forward and comparisons begin to be made. A difference between boys and girls is realized, but not understood. The big difference, to the growing child, is the genitals, thus the reason for this part of the body getting so much attention. The child is really finding out just where he belongs.

**Homosexual:** Boys like boys and girls like girls. "I hate boys (girls)," is often heard during this stage. Roughly speaking this stage covers ages nine through twelve. This involves forming friendships but does not involve sexual desires. It simply means boys gravitate toward boys and girls toward girls, reflecting a normal stage of their development.

**Heterosexual:** They here are moving out of the homosexual stage and an interest in the opposite sex suddenly begins to blossom. "My boy friend" or "My girl friend" is an often heard statement at this point. Such remarks may have been heard during the genital stage, but would have faded as the homosexual stage approached, only to shoot forth again and with more fervor. They really think they have it made here!

I want to stress, once again, that a child does not all at once move out of one stage into another. There is much over-lapping with two or even more of these stages. Neither space nor plans permit a detailed discussion of these stages, but parents need to be aware of their existence. How very helpful it would be if parents could learn some of the characteristics and expectations for each of these stages. Children need help to move smoothly from one stage to another. However, many do not get so smoothly through!

### Fixations

Some children may not completely get out of one stage as they should. When this happens, it is called a *fixation*. This may happen when some need, desire, or goal is blocked or not satisfied. Perhaps I can illustrate with a couple of these stages. A common sign of a fixation in the sucking stage is the child having to have something in his mouth all the time (blanket, thumb, etc.). One of the reasons why some people smoke is thought to be such fixation. I mentioned this possibility once in a lecture, and a grandfather remarked, "I know that would not apply to me, because I didn't start smoking until I was twenty-five years old." He had completely missed the point on fixation. Fixations do not have to show up in childhood, but may appear at any point along life's pathways. They are, however, more likely to show up during the earlier growing years. Adults are often just babies—magnified; and they will do, in more sophisticated ways, just what children often do. A fixation in the homosexual stage is what gives us, in part, the homosexual problems in our society today. Parents failing to understand this may well add to the homosexual list. A cover-up job is often done by parents when they notice that their children have certain homosexual tendencies. Tears will not remove the problem! A word of encouragement is in order—These tendencies can usually be completely cured when caught early enough. Time is important! Consult your doctor at the very first indication of such tendencies in your teenage child. Perhaps many of us who consider ourselves to be adults should reconsider our own growth processes.

## Chapter 6

# NEUROSIS

"Neurosis" is a word used to describe a person whom we call a *neurotic*. "Neurosis" is defined as "disorganized thinking, character-ized by a great deal of anxiety." There are, of course, more than one kind of neurotic, but we shall consider, and that only briefly, the most common approaches to the subject. Neurosis normally arises out of problems involving sex, religion, or inter-personal relations. The following are common factors in most neurotics:

1. Anxiety (see Chapter III)
2. A feeling of being inadequate
3. A feeling of being inferior
4. Tension
5. Being self-centered
6. A lack of insight (not understanding self)
7. Being very rigid (not flexible)
8. Poor relations with others
9. Dissatisfaction and unhappiness
10. Tired, fatigue, and similar complaints

This is not to say that a person who possesses one or more of these qualities is a neurotic. However, we should recognize any of these as a danger signal, suggesting that we are headed in the direction of becoming a neurotic. It should be noted, also, that neu-rosis may progress through different stages, making it extremely difficult to know just when one has really become a neurotic. Be-ing aware of the danger signals, however, should assist us in our observations and make it easier for us to obtain help before the problem can fully develop. However, this is only one side of the coin. Suppose we take a look at the other side and notice how we can develop the three L's: LLL=Live, Laugh, and Love.

For positive mental health I suggest the following:

1. Face reality
2. Concentrate (think seriously)
3. Keep the mind directed forward
4. Have interests outside ourselves
5. Keep lines of communication open
6. Develop a sense of humor
7. Control emotions
8. Have friends
9. Develop a philosophy (a system of values)

The question may be: Just how am I to do all this? I assure you it is not easy. It is often difficult to get people to face reality, to accept facts as facts. This is especially true when those facts would make us uncomfortable. We have every right to expect an adult to work at developing these traits, but children will need help. Again, looking through the eyes of an adult, permit me to suggest a constructive *how* to develop these characteristics. The following chart may help.

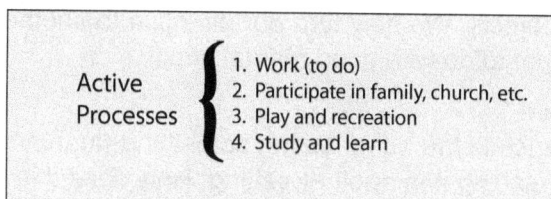

Active Processes {
1. Work (to do)
2. Participate in family, church, etc.
3. Play and recreation
4. Study and learn
}

The above activities will do at least two things. First, as can be seen, they will lead to a fuller and more constructive life. Secondly, they will result in controlled emotions. This second result deals directly with good mental health, and is one of the reasons for this book's being written.

## Suicide

Suicide may not be thought of as important to the purposes of this book, but it does have something to do with good mental health. Also, I have had an increasing number of people calling my attention to statements made by both adults and youngsters expressing intents toward suicide. From a bulletin published in California, "Suicide has been described as coming from within the individual rather than from without, the terminal act being a complicated interaction of psychic events." For 2006 the rate of suicide, nationally was 10.9 for every 100,000 population. Statistics show that the number of teenage suicides are on the increase, thus this may become a problem to some of our children. A few brief comments, then, may be in order.

Three factors that are nearly always present in every real suicide are: A desire to die, a desire to kill, and hate. All three of these being present would make a person a very good candidate for suicide. In the absence of either one of these three, a person is not likely to commit suicide. Of course, from this it would be seen that many deaths that are listed as suicide would not be real suicide. A person may start out just to frighten someone or to get more attention, and he may go further than originally intended and take his own life. This "accidental suicide" does not lessen the grief, but we can see that such is the result of a different kind of a problem, and it can be dealt with in a different way from the causes behind a real suicide.

The real prevention to suicide is, of course, in getting such a person to be a devoted Christian. This is true because Christianity removes both the desire to kill and hate, or, at least, directs them to the proper objects. We now turn our attention to another topic that has somewhat to do with good mental health.

## Transference

Transference is the act of taking something (mentally) from one setting and placing it in another setting. How does this work in human relations? First, let me suggest that this is a constant process in both young and old. This is the act of seeing someone who is very much like someone whom you have known before. It is the transferring of your feelings from someone in your past to someone in your present. When someone reminds us, because of some trait or traits, of someone we have known in the past. These reminders may be good or bad. Have you ever thought, why do I dislike him (her)? Or, why do I like him (her)? And, the answer may well be because of this thing which we call transference. But, let us pursue this a little deeper into these human relations.

Should little Jane remind you of a resented aunt, some or all of your feelings concerning that particular aunt may well be directed at little Jane. As a youngster you may have disliked some particular relative, neighbor, or an acquaintance. Should one of your own children display a trait of this disliked person, that child could come in for some stormy reactions from you. One young married woman confided in me that she was having difficulty in keeping lady friends, but simply did not know why. Further conversation revealed that she had poor relations with just about every woman that was part of her past life—as a youngster. The possibility of transference in these cases was found to be of real value. Now, suppose that you are in this position! At the same time, the person to whom you are relating is experiencing the same thing. Do you think the two of you will ever become friends? Is this really fair to either of you? Now, do you see the importance of making as sure as possible that our children develop healthy relationships as they grow up?

However, transference need not all be bad. It is possible for this to work when we are reminded of some wonderful person in our past. There is a danger here, however, of our showering affection or attention upon a child that reminds us of such a person, to the exclusion of another child—and this last child would feel hurt, neglected, or unwanted. We need to be aware of possible transference, that we might be more objective when dealing with other people. Facing the facts here will make a real contribution to good healthy relationships throughout our lives.

One more helpful thought here; transference may be with reference to someone (or traits) who is real, or with someone (or traits) who is not real but imagined. People often need help to overcome the bad aspects of transference, especially is this true of a growing youngster.

# Chapter 7

# PARENTS

Parents often operate on the pleasure—pain principle; that is, making the punishment fit the crime. That appears, even from a Bible viewpoint, to be a good principle—good, if we do not forget the other side of the coin! That other side says that the praise (a form of encouragement) should fit the good deeds of the child. Now, we note four common kinds of parents, with a brief comment on each.

1. **Over-Indulgent Parent.** This is primarily a means of pleasure to the parent and not to the child. It also avoids the responsibility of teaching the child proper values.

2. **Over-Permissive Parent.** This attempts to avoid having the child unpleasant or unhappy, and avoids the chance of having the child withdraw his approval of the parent. "He will hate me" is often the thought of the over-permissive parent.

3. **Over-Protective Parent.** The parent is here avoiding discomfort or inconvenience. He does this by focusing attention upon the risk being taken.

4. **Over-Expective Parent.** This parent hopes to avoid the child's way of thinking, acting, or feeling. The parent desires to have the child to think, act, and feel as does the parent.

What are the dangers of being an over-expective parent? The following are some of the possible effects (on the child) of an over-expective parent:

1. Feeling of inadequacy
2. Anxiety
3. Feeling of insecurity

4. A feeling of dependence

5. A fear of failure

6. A fear of the loss of approval

7. An inferiority complex

8. A feeling of guilt

9. A feeling of being rejected

10. A lack of self confidence

11. A fear of risk

12. A weak ego structure (don't forget conflicts and fixations here)

## Discipline

Discipline may be thought of as *gaining control of behavior*. At birth a child starts out almost completely under his parents' control. The idea of discipline is to so control the child that he will need less and less control by the parent, and will have more and more control of himself. The following picture will illustrate how that we are never, completely, out from under the control of others.

In spite of our efforts to properly control and direct the behavior of the child, things still sometimes go wrong. Here are a few suggestions that are good remedial measures.

1. Make sure that rules and limitations are thoroughly understood.

2. Children can often suggest good workable rules.

Control by others / Control by self — Infancy ... Maturity

3. Perhaps a number of things can be tried before overt punishment.

4. Use action instead of words (guidance with firmness).

5. There is no need of humiliation. One aim is to get them to grow up thinking well of themselves.

6. When punishment is necessary it must accomplish something. Otherwise it is useless and harmful.

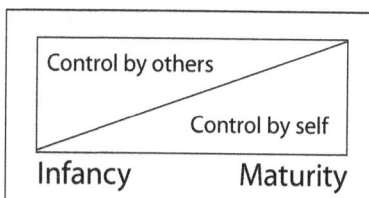

7.  Whatever we do, we must ask—*Does this improve the child? Does it change his attitudes, etc.?*

# Chapter 8

# PROBLEMS OF CHILDREN

## In General

*There is no such thing as a problem child!* Sound strange? There are children with problems, but no such things as a problem child. There is a difference. A big difference! To view the child as a problem child invites attack on the child instead of the child's problem and could cause a resentment of the child and preclude a solution of any problem which may be present. Nearly two thousand years ago the Roman Philosopher, Epictetus, observed, "Men are not disturbed by things, but by the view which they take of them."

Whether we are parents, teachers, or merely acquaintances— *What really disturbs us when we are around children*? Is it the child, or is it the view we take of the child? Broaden this just a little and ask—when a child or circumstances disturb you, is it really the child or circumstances? Perhaps our view of such children or circumstances is really the disturber. You may ask, what else do I have to rely on? And, I add, that is a good question and I do not, here, offer an answer. However, I do challenge you to reevaluate your view of things. When that reevaluation is done, we may be able to laugh at ourselves just a little. And, I might add, it just might be that we will then become more constructive in the rearing or training of the child.

All children have the same *basic needs*. The tangible needs are such things as food, clothing, and shelter. The intangible needs of love, a feeling of belonging, a feeling of being needed or wanted, a feeling of adequacy, and a feeling of self-esteem are the needs most often overlooked. It is the responsibility of parents to supply these needs to their growing children. You will notice that I use the word parents (plural). The father who expects the mother to supply all these needs is making a serious mistake. Such excuses as, "I'm too busy," "I just don't have time," or "I'm too tired," are made by fathers who, generally, do not want the responsibility. Perhaps they don't feel capable of handling the situation and don't want to admit their fear. We should remember the conflicts of Chapter II and IV. "Problem parents" beget "problem children." When parents recognize their own problems and do something about them, they are going to rear children with fewer problems.

*Whatever a child does has meaning!* It may reveal his *needs*, his *desires*, or even *emotional disturbances*. When a child reacts in some unusual way, the wise parent or teacher will silently ask, "What caused this?" Most of the time a little thought and observation will bring a ready answer. However, the right answer is not always easy. To illustrate just how difficult to understand the inner workings of a child can be sometimes, let me cite a case given by a physiologist many years ago: A little boy wanted the undivided love of his mother and he resented his father as a rival. He felt guilty about his feelings toward his father, and, at the same time he feared what his father would do to him. Such anxiety, over a period of time, provoked some reaction from the boy. He became afraid of open spaces and horses. This fear enabled him to stay indoors near his mother. Transferring some of his fear from his father to the horse made it possible for him to tolerate his father around his mother without an unreasonable fear. You see, it can become rather complex at times; and professional help may be desirable. Parents, when you do not have the answer, get that professional help! A sense of guilt, anxiety, fear, hostility, or hate may cause mental illness. Do we really want our children to grow up, having good mental health?

To various groups I have often asked, "When does a child most need parental love?" Answers have been about as varied as the circumstances. Yet, just a little reflection will bring the simple answer—When he is least loved! As parents we need to think seriously about the implications of this simple answer. How often do we really see the child as he really is? Do we have some pet personality peeve that prevents us from seeing our child as he is? Perhaps we see the child within the realm of our own expectations of him, rather than in the realm of his own feelings and potentials. Rigid expectations which we have of our children, husbands, wives, and others may well become a prison for us and ruin what otherwise could have been a happy relationship.

Parents or teachers are usually concerned with many problems relating to children: When a child hurts another child, when a child is destructive, when a child uses bad language, when a child won't share, when a child still sucks his thumb, just to name a few. From the child's viewpoint both parents and teachers are often inconsistent in dealings with the problems of the child. Permit an illustration. Problem: A child flings a doll across the room.

| Action | Parental Response |
|---|---|
| 1. Doll lands on soft chair | 1. No comment |
| 2. Doll breaks | 2. Child is scolded for being destructive and told that he should not be given nice things |
| 3. Doll hits an expensive vase and breaks it | 3. Child is punished for being destructive |

Parental response here appeared perfectly proper from the parents' point of view, but what about the child? To him all he did was to toss a doll across the room. Do we expect the child to understand our actions as if he was already an adult? Do we take the time to be sure that the child understands why we do certain things in certain ways?

It should be pointed out once again that *at no time is a child completely at his chronological age.* He is most often a mixture of the past, present, and even future. There will be over-lapping in his development. He will grow more rapidly in some ways than in others. All this is normal, but parents need to recognize this fact when dealing with the growing child.

**Tools of the Trade**

Where are we at this point? In the short chapters through which you have passed, I have tried to give you what might be called "tools." These tools are offered, for the most part, in terms of mental processes. One might decide to become a builder, a construction specialist. Such would need some tools, and he would need to know just how to use those tools. As he used those tools again and again, he would become more and more effective in their use. He, perhaps

had to have assistance when he began using the tools, but he could soon use them without much assistance. The constant and thoughtful use of his tools produced the kind of progress with which he would be delighted.* I offer you, then, this "box of tools" and I sincerely trust that you will make a most effective use of them—the more the use, the brighter they shine!

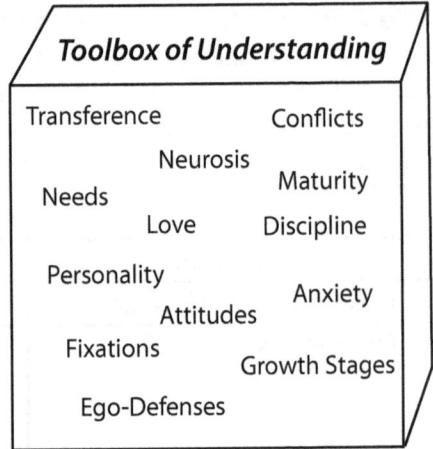

**Toolbox of Understanding**

Transference          Conflicts

Neurosis

Needs                         Maturity

Love          Discipline

Personality

Attitudes                    Anxiety

Fixations

Growth Stages

Ego-Defenses

There they are, box and all! What shall you do with them? Shall they rust away, unused? Prepare! Preparing! Prepared! I recall reading a little story told by the late President of the coal-miners union, John L. Lewis: Two miners had an argument. One was better educated than the other. Finally, they decided that the only way to settle the argument was with their fists. The better educated one suggested that the first one to get enough would say "Sufficient," and the other readily agreed. They battled each other for about thirty minutes or so, first one and then the other rolling with the blows. Finally, the better educated one a little hesitantly, but plainly, called out, "Sufficient!" The other fellow picked himself up from the dust, shook off his clothes, wiped the blood from his nose, and said, "I have been trying to think of that word for a half hour!" Moral? Prepare!

As you move through the longest chapter, the next one, I trust that you shall find proper use for all these tools of understanding, and that you will become a very effective parent in so doing. You owe your child no less, and God demands that you accept the responsibility (Eph. 6:4; Col. 3:21).

# Chapter 9

# UNDERSTANDING THE CHILD

"But the wisdom that is from above is first pure, then peaceable, gentle, and easy to be entreated, full of mercy and good fruits, without partiality, and without hypocrisy" (Jas. 3:17). The attributes of heavenly wisdom are here set forth in simple terms. There is no substitute for this wisdom! Fortunate is the child who has a parent who is a dedicated child of God—better still, whose father and mother both are faithful children of God. Such a parent(s) will not only be concerned, but will constantly be alert as to how they might be more effective as parents. Please reread the above quoted passage. I challenge each parent to honestly ask themselves: Is this the wisdom that characterizes my relationship with my child? While we are told to pray for wisdom (Jas. 1:5), God does not promise to "pump" one's idle mind full of that wisdom. We simply must learn to apply ourselves, to give any situation our best. *Knowledge* is defined as that which we may acquire through study and observation. *Wisdom* is that trait about us that enables us to best use that knowledge. This is true of either adult or child.

Educators often list what they call **The Four Language Skills**, and here they are:

```
1. Reading ———— Intake Skills
2. Writing
3. Speaking ———— Outgoing Skills
4. Listening
```

You will notice that #'s 1 and 4 are the intake skills, the way we take in information, while #'s 2 and 3 are the outgoing skills, the way we put out information. We need to realize that we simply cannot "put out" what we do not "take in." This point has an excellent application to both parents and children. If parents want to "put out" what is necessary to properly rear children, somewhere along the line they must "take in" that which is necessary. If parents desire that their children be able to "put out" what is necessary to succeed in life, they must accept the responsibility in seeing to it that those children "take in"—another way of saying that they must accept the responsibility to *teach* and *train* their children. Yes, parents, God gave you that responsibility!

It should be understood that *thinking* is required along with each of those language skills, regardless of who may be the user. Rote memory of information is not enough. Just as memorizing the Scriptures is not enough (within itself) to make one acceptable to God, so it is with the information necessary in rearing a child—*it must be applied!*

## From Birth to Five Years

During this period the child is almost completely dependent upon his parents. He is closer to those parents, during this period, than at any other time. His world is small, but *not* unimportant. I well remember an experience with my own son. When he was about three years of age, he was taken on a trip which required some overnight driving. After riding all night (asleep), he awoke and immediately wanted to go to the bathroom. This was a perfectly normal reaction and we would immediately care for his need (so we thought). He insisted we return home for him to use the bathroom! To him it should have been no difficulty at all—just turn around and drive back home! It took a while to get him to see that we could not do that, and I am not sure we succeeded. However, nature forced his compliance. His small world was easily understood, and it was difficult for him to accept the enlarged world of the adult. A mother or father (or both) is constantly with the child during this time, and they somehow get the idea that they understand that child. Without meaning to question the ability of any parent, I ask the question, *do you really understand your child*? Let us see!

From birth to five years the needs of a child are limited, but those needs have an ever-widening edge. The child begins, at birth, to react to the world about him (including his parents). His first sound which we hear is usually the result of a "swatted" bottom—a loud cry. From that moment on he learns better and better how to use that sound for his own advantage. His mother, at first, is just one great big bag of milk! It would insult some mothers to realize that this is the way a child first views them. But, the alert mother keeps watching; and anxiously waiting for that first sign—"See, he knows his mother, already!" But, what is the child thinking? The mother, at feeding time, caresses, rocks, or otherwise gives the child attention. Soon the child learns—"not bad, not bad; if I cry a little, look what I get!" He enjoys all this attention (which is normal) and he learns just how to get more of it, improving his techniques all along. There isn't anything wrong with desiring attention, and a proper balance is the desired goal. Even so, here begins the age-old battle: Does the child control the parent, or does the parent control the child? The child has no sense of responsibility here, but the parents most certainly should have.

Closeness develops which the concerned parent hopes will last a lifetime. *It can, but will it?* Much to the dismay of many parents the answer will be, no! But, why should this be so? God did not determine it that way, nor does the child so determine. Who, then, shall determine such? Unwittingly, many parents make this determination when they fail to prepare themselves to be parents, when they are indifferent to their responsibilities as parents, or when they simply do not care. God said, "But if any provide not for his own, and specially for those of his own house, he hath denied the faith, and is worse than an infidel" (1 Tim. 5:8). It is a sad mistake to conclude that the only necessary provisions are food, clothing, and shelter. It is often suggested that, if elders are to properly feed the flock (Acts 20:28), they must have some understanding of the flock. I think most of the members of the church would consider this a valid point. Is it not just as true in supplying the complete needs of a growing child? We must somehow acquire an understanding of the child and his needs.

One young mother recently said to me, "I prepared myself to be the mother of a baby and not the mother of a teenager." I am persuaded that this mother spoke the truth for a great many parents. Parents will, normally, understand the needs of a child at and soon after birth. They will also have a pretty good idea of how to meet those needs. But, as that child grows the situation becomes more complex. A young father who, because of a death, had become the adopted father of two teenagers, said, "It is not easy for a father to grow up so fast." His point is well taken. A good understanding of the growing child doesn't come easily, but only after much dedicated effort. Is it worth it? The finished product well answers that question. How will it answer that question for you? Have you been a successful parent? Have you failed? What will the answer be?

## Ages Five and Six

At ages five or six the picture begins to change. The child is shared with teachers and an increased number of companions. Less and less time is spent at home with parents or other members of the family. At school he mixes with his peers, and he is like them in many ways. Yet, he is different in many other ways: Is he an orphan child, an only child, from a broken home or stable home? Is he from a large house or small apartment? Are his parents young or middle-aged? Is his home situation poor or comfortable? Is his home stable or highly transient? What is his race? Religion, if any? Any one of these factors or a combination of them can make your child very different from other children.

How is the child going to respond to others, as he is thrown together with them? Remember how attitudes are set? (See Chapter IV.) Since attitudes are set by *training* and *experience*, he will react to others in exactly the way his training and experience tell him to act. So, you see, the first five years with his parents have prepared him to begin with success or with failure! Which shall it be?

Someone has correctly observed that when a child leaves home for the first time (to school, etc.), he leaves with a pack of troubles on his back. Some of these packs may be no larger than your fist, but others are just heavier than the child can carry; he can hardly move beneath the weight. How do we get a peek into or inside this bag of troubles? If we only knew, we could more easily meet the challenge of supplying his needs. Is there some way we can tell what these troubles are? The child is not, then, able to tell us. Perhaps we shall never know, completely. This should not, however, prevent us from finding out all that we can. *Get this: Parents, that pack of troubles never leaves your child!* The content may vary from time to time, but it will always be there. Because it seems fitting, I shall offer one simple suggestion at this point. Did you ever watch your child play house with other children? Please don't pass up the opportunity if you ever have one. If you really want to see how you really look to the child, secretly watch him play house. You will likely get a pretty good idea of how you impress him.

How do others view that child? What about the teacher, when she sees a child come into her room for the very first time? The burden of teaching (with its wide scope) will often cause the teacher to view the child as just another child who, somehow, must be fit into the curriculum involved in her room. Do Sunday school teachers do the same thing? What about parents? Is each child just another child who somehow must be made to fit among other members of the family? What, now, really disturbs the teacher or parent? Is it the child, or is it their view of him?

Let us escort the child from school back to his home and see what happens. A kind and cooperative child may have suddenly become ruthless and uncooperative. He may cheat or steal. He may lie (to avoid punishment). He may be disorderly and defiant, or he may pilfer and fail to keep his promises. The parent wonders, "What in the world has happened to my child, what has school done to him?" "He is now rebellious!" "He is greedy for things and careless with them once they are his." "He is ready for a 'tug-of-war' with just about any member of the family." Revolt? Rebellion? Against what? As strange as it may seem, it is revolt or rebellion against parental love, parental control, and parental standards. Again, as strange as it may seem, he is going through a normal period of growth. Under such circumstances parents often become frustrated and uncertain, and often overlook the better side. One confused mother angrily accused her small son of not keeping his promises, breaking his word, and he replied, "But I have a lot of unbroken words left."

Now, I invite you to visit the school situation again with this child. We observe different classroom behavior. IQ's of the children are different. Some are slow, and others are fast. Some large, others small. Some are eager and some are lazy; some babyish while others are maturing normally. We see some aggressive and others withdrawing. The teacher knows that some will like her while others may even hate her. Others may merely be suspicious. Here the child soon learns that *it is easier to go along, to conform to the routine of his peers*, than to oppose such. He dislikes being pressed or pushed. Parents, right here begins some future problems—the idea of going along with the crowd!

Conflicts can easily arise between teacher and parent. Teachers may sometimes wonder just what the home is doing to the child. One teacher, being rebuked by an angry parent, was heard to say, "If you won't believe all he tells you about me, I won't believe all he tells me about you." Most of the time, parents who really understand their children will recognize this as a pretty good deal.

I well remember a most wonderful and understanding kindergarten teacher, while I was serving as a public school administrator. It became almost daily routine for her to come by my office once she had dismissed her class for the day; here she would relate to me some of the interesting experiences of the morning. These normally included some of the sayings of the children. I kept a file on these, and they still provide some interesting reading. One youngster provided an interesting sidelight when he became frustrated at not being able to perform certain tasks. Pounding his fists on the table he said, "I got just too much dumb!"

Our journey is not complete until we go back home with this child, once more. Remember the over-expective parents? Here at home the child learns that his parents give or withhold their love to the degree that the child fits into their expectations. Parents have become disappointed because he has not become the child of their dreams; and, these parents may often hold up the brother or sister as an example to the child. And, the child may wonder, "Why can't I be just me, instead of like someone else?"

Why have I taken you back and forth, from home to school to home? I am trying to show you the difficulty the child faces, and he lacks the experience and training with which to make sound judgments. Yet, he does not like to have demands placed upon him. He cannot, yet, see things through the eyes of an adult, while adult behavior is often expected of him. At this point you may feel like the young lad that was asked to define space, "Well, it's like where there's nothing, I can't define it very well, but I got it in my head all right!" *Trying to understand the child is the main point!*

What is going on in the mind of the child during this time? Ideas of "fair" and "unfair" are taking shape. Fears often form that tarry with the child for extended periods—perhaps for years, or even life. Friends are a most important acquisition of the child during this period, and he is often very jealous of his friends. Here are some of his worries:

1. He wonders whether or not his parents accept and approve of him.

2. Is he unwanted or unloved?

3. Any change which he must make, may be unsettling.

4. He is envious of his more fortunate peers and it is difficult sometimes for him to play with them.

5. Death is sometimes a child's worry.

6. The young child has age-appropriate sex curiosity, such as ideas of "sissy" or "tomboy."

7. Marriage may worry the child, especially if there are marital problems in the home.

8. Money matters. These may become a child's concern, partly through the overhearing of what parents are saying.

9. Children often fear the dark, thunder, doctors, etc.

10. Friends become a concern of the typical child—he wants one for his very own.

His friends: Why don't children understand parental disapproval of their choice of friends? The child thinks in terms of "now" and not in "long-range" plans. The parent, of course, thinks just the opposite. Unguarded remarks of parents may injure their relationship with the child: "So-and-so is dirty," "I wonder who his father is," etc. A child may choose a friend of whom the parents do not approve as an act of rebellion against the parents. Yet, there are many factors which affect these friendships: time, distance, traffic, and many others. Such factors often preclude the child being able to continue his desired friendship. In what ways can the parent assist the child through this stage of growth?

During this stage *competition* among children is very strong; and for three basic reasons:

1. He is trying to find a place for himself.

2. He wants admiration.

3. He needs to feel successful at something.

Are there ways in which we as parents or teachers can help the child in achieving these three things?

One final point before leaving this age bracket. From birth to six years is the most flexible age of the child. If we are wise, we will take an advantage of this flexibility. We will be trying to mold the thinking, the behavior, the standards, and the attitudes of that child—that they be constructive and not destructive. Above all, here is the period in which you can do some very effective teaching and character building based upon God's Word. Later may well be too late! Should we fail to take advantage of this early age, we may begin to feel like the new secretary who remarked, "I don't see how I have done it; I have been here ten days and I am already twenty days behind."

## The Seven Year Old

As we approach the seven-year-old child, we have an advantage. We have learned something about his makeup; we have received a limited peek into his pack of troubles and we have some sense of the direction in which we must move. His pack of troubles may vary at this point. But he still has them. He will have moved some of his troubles from his pack, but he will have added more. We face a new challenge, but we are better prepared.

The seven year old grows more slowly than at five or six. One year more experience brings some changes in his behavior and reactions. He begins to question "authority," both at home and at school. He has learned how to please and displease, and he takes full advantage of this new found power. It becomes a weapon which he often uses to reach his desired ends. And, another chief weapon is that of name-calling, and he wastes no time in using it to the fullest. The words or names which he uses may often mean absolutely nothing to him; his choice will likely be based on what the words accomplish—does he get to do what he wants? Does he get his way? Does he get the attention which he desires? His rebellion may be more pronounced and will often shift from home to school. He is testing to see just where his rebellion will be of greatest advantage to him.

This is also the age of "tall tales." This is perfectly normal and should be so understood. The reaction of parents and others to this normal reaction of the child may often do harm. Remember our discussion on the subject of *fixations*? Be careful lest we react with too much alarm and make too may demands. Enjoy (with the child) this period of great imaginations! As you might well understand, *dramatic play* reaches its peak in the child's life at about this point. Doesn't this suggest something as to how we might help the child properly grow toward maturity?

Personal friends are still important to him, but he is more compatible with his peers. Have you ever wondered why pets are so important to a child of this age? Pets become extremely important to a child of this age because they furnish an outlet for the child's love. He feels more *secure* in this love than with parental love. Why? Pets do not withdraw their love as some parents may do. Further, their love of the pet is fully reciprocated by the pet. Does this give you a hint, parents?

A child of this age may revert (in both thinking and acting) to an earlier age of comfort, if he cannot throw off some of the pressures or worries of this age. His progress, then, may well depend on the assistance which he gets from parents and others—that he might successfully move on through this period of development. His feelings are shown in different ways: thumb-sucking, nail biting, bed wetting, etc. Parents should take such reactions as danger signals and look for the cause. To try to stop such reactions without seeking the cause behind them, will often drive the child to a different kind of reaction and does not solve the problem. These are merely symptoms, suggesting the presence of a problem with which the child has not been able to successfully cope. Parents, watch for such danger signals, find out what is behind them, and do what you can to remove them. We now leave the seven year old, with his pack of troubles, but we find him again, a little more advanced, in . . .

## The Eight Year Old

He hasn't lost his pack of troubles; we see a few more changes in the content, but the pack is about as full as it was last year. He has added one more year's experience, and some new horizons begin to appear.

He is more conscious of his appearance, as well as the appearance of others. This consciousness may well prove to be the problem, for he will begin to make comparisons between himself and others. He may wonder why the differences. It is important here that he is pleased with his own appearance; and, he takes special note of approval or disapproval of his appearance by others, especially his peers. He begins to idolize older people with whom he is brought into contact—teachers, older brothers or sisters, policemen, garbage men; and, in this day of constant television viewing, a few T.V. characters may be thrown into this group.

The age of 8 is the age of experimentation, and he has a great curiosity to satisfy. Hint, hint, parents! He can divide between facts and fantasy, and you may often hear him say, "When I was young." A sense of values (money, etc.) is being pretty well formed; not just a difference in two coins, but comparative values. Neither is this value sense limited to oberservable objects, but ideas can be understood. Parents still have the opportunity, at this age, to help mold this still flexible piece of clay. He can develop ideas and he can accept prejudices. He has the ability to recognize and accept the fact that different people feel differently. His world has become greatly enlarged, and he has a greater awareness of people and things that surround him.

The eight year old still holds on to special friends, even longer that the six or seven year old. On the other hand, he is able to share those friends with others without too much pain. Here is a good opportunity to broaden his realm of friends. He can accept races, religions, living standards, all because he has the ability to make comparisons and accept differences. This *idea of comparisons* is one that will stick with him, and during his teens he will really make use of it! His ability to accept differences will not, automatically, erase his feelings when he is on the short end of his comparisons. He will thus need assistance in making adjustments.

## The Nine Year Old

A child does not move from eight to nine as easily as he moved from seven to eight. He is bordering on adolescence and he approaches this period of life with some degree of anxiety. Much like one who may have been jumping the small streams, but suddenly comes to a river—it is approached with mixed emotions and studious caution. He just doesn't know whether or not he wants to move on, and he may not understand (probably doesn't) the things happening to him. If past pressures have been too much for him, they begin to show on the surface: habitual blinking of eyes, coughing, or other physical signs. Such danger signals would suggest that the child is hesitating in the growth process—he hasn't quite successfully met the pressures of the past, and he dislikes the idea of taking on more. Under such circumstances this is a normal reaction; he is merely protecting himself—remember the conflicts and the ego-defense mechanisms. We simply have to learn to get behind those pressures and find out what is causing them, so that the child can look ahead with confidence.

As you may well suppose, the nine year old still has the pack of troubles. Even though the content may be somewhat changed, his pack may be somewhat enlarged, also. The smoothness with which he moved from five to six, from six to seven, and seven to eight, is just not here now. He abruptly comes face to face with some very disturbing things and processes. What are some of those things and processes?

There is a tendency toward being with a group instead of just some special friend. Special friends do not cease to be important, but the stronger feeling is for the group. This calls for adjustment to and the acceptance by a group instead of just one friend, and this can be rather frustrating. He simply does not realize that all other nine year olds are bothered by the same thoughts. This group consciousness is very pronounced, with group games or clubs being the order of the day.

A dangerous "self-consciousness" develops. In other words he will be very much aware of his strengths and his weaknesses. His past failures will likely pass before his face. By comparison, he draws conclusions as to whether he is "ugly" or "attractive," and his physical features such as big feet, large nose, bad teeth, or some deformity all play a big part in the thinking of the nine year old. He usually will set high standards for himself, but has inadequate techniques for accomplishing those standards. This self-consciousness may preclude or block creative work, or even normal learning. His efforts to be successful may be "turned-off" by what he thinks of himself. This process may be a clue for the parent of the child who has been making good grades in school, but now those grades take a dive. Perhaps the same can be said with reference to the child that has adjusted well but now begins to have difficulties in adjusting. His weaknesses or those physical features which he considers to be bad may weigh so heavily in his mind that he withdraws from making normal efforts. We, as teachers or parents, would do well to take emphasis off such things and "play up" the good points or strengths of the child. It is not enough to merely tell the child that such things are not important; we must make him feel that in spite of those things, he is still a worthwhile and respected individual, that he is loved and wanted.

The nine year old will identify himself with modern heroes. He does not, as the eight year old, merely idolize the hero, but he identifies himself with such heroes. In other words, he may now think of himself as playing the role of his hero, to the point that he may actually try to do some of the same things. Since these heroes may be taken from movies, T.V., comic books, baseball, or any "in" activity of the day, parents can see how problematic this characteristic of the nine year old can really be. In fact, he may choose his hero as an act of defiance of parental choices. This is one good reason for parents to "go easy" in affirming their choices with the nine year old. It may well backfire! Even a compliment which you pay to some other youngster in the presence of the nine year old may be taken as an insult—"You like him better than you like me" or "I'm a failure." Intended? Certainly not, but the nine year old neither reads nor understands your intentions. Nor, do you have the right to expect him to fully understand; he is just not capable yet. For this reason the nine year old may need a little extra attention; and most certainly needs your compliments. Such can provide the extra assurance which he needs during this stage of his growth.

Parents, you are about to leave behind the last *real chance* which you have at molding the thinking and habits of your child. True, you can still exert a good influence in their lives on through the teen years, but your influence on the teen is going to be more limited. Further, much of that you may accomplish during the teen years will depend on the job which you have done up through age nine. If you have not had a good relationship with your child up through age nine, it will normally mean disaster for the child and heart-break for the parent. Why is this so?

As the child passes through this age bracket, he begins to enter the *homosexual stage* of development. Now, what does this mean? Take another look at chapter V. The child begins to like his own sex better than the opposite sex, and somewhere around age ten he has fully entered this stage. Up to this point the opposite is true—he liked the opposite sex better. After entering the homosexual stage, little Jane couldn't care less whether she has a good relationship with her father or not. And, little Johnny couldn't careless whether or not he has a good relationship with his mother. Here is the stage when boys like boys and girls like girls. "I hate boys," or "I hate girls," is often heard during the homosexual stage. And, they will stay in this homosexual stage for some two or three years-depending upon the child. I have introduced some discussion of the homosexual stage at this place because this is where the change begins to occur. A further discussion of the homosexual stage in the next section will extend our thinking on this point.

However, I want to give emphasis, once again, to the fact—and it is a fact *from birth up through age nine is the time for you to make your best and most lasting impressions upon the child.* You are going to make impressions and these impressions are going to last—will they be good or bad? What kind of contributions are you making to the future of your child? If parents could be made to see the importance of these first nine years, perhaps many disasters could be avoided.

Through the last four paragraphs I have attempted to discuss some of those processes that so often disturb the nine year old child. I sincerely trust that such discussion has given you a better insight into your child of this age. I have no desire to be shocking; yet, I think the implications of the last four paragraphs should be shocking to parents. Can parents not realize that during these first nine years they are training either good contributing citizens, or delinquents, criminals, or parasites? It would be a mistake to pass

up another comparison—that we are either training children to become and live as Christians, or to be an insult to the great Cause of
Christ. Which is it going to be?

## The Ten – Twelve Year Olds

We are here looking at children who for the most part are in the
homosexual stage. Their packs of troubles may appear to be con-
siderably smaller since they do not seem to affect parents quite
so much as earlier difficulties. Do not let this appearance fool you;
those troubles or problems are there, just awaiting the time of expo-
sure—just a little more development of the youngster. The child is
physically pretty well developed, but he is still a child.

It is during these years that the ideas of "younger set" and "older
set" take shape, and they become pretty well marked during this
time. Groups of the "younger set" may gang up on the "older set";
they are testing their strength. And, they feel much more obligated
to follow the standard of their peers than that of their parents. Before this, they may have found it easier to go along with their peers,
but now they feel obligated to do so! Parents need to know that this
is a normal feeling for this age, that it is not just rebellion, as such.
Nonetheless, it will produce some problems. If parents have had
a good relationship with the child up to this point, the task will be
much easier. Should the opposite be true, this period will become
increasingly difficult. Consistency and fairness, as always, is very
important here. Firmness is no less important, but parents need to
do some thinking before they begin making too many demands.
"Haste makes waste" could not be truer here.

Being responsible or non-responsible is very noticeable during this
age. In fact, along about here, a child may often appear to have lost
all sense of responsibility—even though he was very dependable
earlier in life. Believe it or not, the child of this age normally wants
responsibility. The reason for this apparent conflict in the child's feelings is the fact that he desires to be useful and important, and he
must prove himself—to himself, as well as to others. Wise parents
will make use of this desire to be useful and important, assigning
tasks that will help him meet these needs. The child of this age will
likely resent being assigned tasks which he has "out-grown." "I'm not
a child any more" is a frequent retort to those assignments which
they feel to be childish, and this is serious business with the child.

Just as the nine year old is beginning to enter the homosexual stages, the ten – twelve year old (most likely eleven or twelve) is beginning to move out of the homosexual stage and into the heterosexual stage. They may begin to mimic older brothers or sisters, or even friends that are older, with such ideas as "going steady." Here is where the "fur" really begins to fly between child and parent. There is no necessity of reminding parents of a teenager of all the ups and downs that can happen about here.

One thing is extremely important here, more so than at any earlier time—*keep the channels of communication open!* Often *discussion* with these children is more important than the *information* which you may give them. This is not to say that it may be proper to give them the wrong information, but it is to say that you should not be too concerned if circumstances do not permit you to give the child all the information which you may think that he needs. If the channels of communication are kept open, continued chances will be yours. Close that channel and you get nothing through. Basically, it is the responsibility of the parent to keep such channels open; the child does not, yet, understand the importance. The child is going to demand—in words or actions—more freedom than the parent is willing to give. It is very easy to close that channel at this point!

Parents who take the attitude that they will make their child sit down and listen to what they have to say have something to learn. You may force him to sit and to look at you, but you cannot force him to think about what you have to say. Voluntary deafness is the child's weapon at this point; you don't really get through to him under such circumstances. Again, I point out, that if your past relationship with the child has been good, this part is made easier. Is it such a crime for a parent to realize that he might be wrong? You may find it profitable to deal with your child, keeping in mind this possibility. Children may, and often do, suggest rules and regulations that are both practical and workable. Why not give him a chance? He may surprise you!

Children of this age bracket are really standing in a "doorway" between two extremes:

1. Looking ahead and rushing too quickly toward adult complex behavior.

2.  Looking back and just sticking with younger children to escape the unpleasantness of this age with its problems and responsibilities.

Beware, lest we force them to either extreme. Every child has a right to be permitted to grow up, to grow up in a normal way. As parents we need to (figuratively) take our child by the hand, and lead him through the dangers of growing up, guiding him around the pitfalls of life. After having done this, and when he comes to the point at which he "steps out on his own" to make his life with another, our tears will be expressions of happiness and not of sorrow. You will have discharged the obligation that God long ago placed upon all parents, and this can be one of those things about which you can hear Him say, in judgment, "Well done, thy good and faithful servant."

# Chapter 10

# SOME CLOSING THOUGHTS

Every child, as he moves through his growth stages, will have a rather lengthy list of needs. At the very top of any such list is *love*. Love, properly manifested, will cover a multitude of ills. Every child has a right to the devoted love of his parents. This is a love that properly cares for the child, properly directs the child, and properly leads the child. True love does not become over-permissive, over indulgent, over-protective, nor over-expective (see chapter VII).

Rating a healthy second on any list of needs is *understanding*. This, of course, is the design of this book. It has not been my design to offer numerous remedies for the problems mentioned or implied; these have intentionally been kept to a minimum. I have simply tried to help you better understand your child. In the writing of this book, I have assumed that parents are sufficiently intelligent to apply the remedies, once they understand the need. Parents who love their child will seek out and apply the proper remedies. However, remedies are of little or no value unless the parent has a fair understanding of the child and his needs.

There are no "set" rules nor "pat" answers to the problems that will arise in the rearing of children. Such will vary child to child, and from time to time. I can offer you two suggestions, which if you follow you will find the rules and answers coming much easier: (1) Love your child, (2) Understand your child. *Encouragement* is both a rule and an answer for many of the problems. A few simple words of encouragement, if offered sincerely, will accomplish a great deal. On this point, I merely repeat what Mark Twain once said, "The difference between right words and wrong words is the difference between lightening bugs and lightening."

A few suggestions for parents may be in order:

1.  Try to be prepared for the unexpected. Learn some of the standard remarks to avoid and some standard things which you might do.

2.  Try to think of given situations and then learn some things which you might say in those situations.

3.  Remember that the unexpected things may include such as sex, tall tales, lies, stealing, etc.

4.  Keep talking things over with the child as much as possible.

5.  Encourage dramatic play and observe as you can.

6.  Plan to share experiences with your children.

7.  Remember! Gifts are not substitutes for love.

8.  Generally speaking, "The fewer the rules the better."

9.  Help your child understand "authority" and the proper respect for that authority: Parental, teachers, laws of the land, and above all, God and His Law, the Bible.

One final suggestion and we shall close our book: Parents, seek help! Do not wait until the "mole-hills" have grown into "mountains." When there are problems for which you do not have a solution, I repeat, seek help. I have had people come desiring my help, but they have waited until it was almost (if not entirely) too late. This causes the problem solving to often be painful, and sometimes prevents a solution completely. There is seldom an easy way out. We cannot wish our problems away! Hopeful wishing may be comforting, but it is not a solution. I am reminded of the story of an old Indian who led his small son to a mountain overlooking a beautiful valley and said, "Some day, my son, all this land will belong to the Indians again. Palefaces all go to the moon."